QED ESSENTIALS

Let's Talk

The Seasons

Flowers grow in the sun in spring.

Animals are born.

We can play in the spring rain!

The Seasons

Simon Mugford

Quarto is the authority on a wide range of topics.

Quarto educates, entertains and enriches the lives of our readers—enthusiasts and lovers of hands-on living.

www.quartoknows.com

© 2019 Quarto Publishing plc

First published in 2019 by QED Publishing,
an imprint of The Quarto Group.
The Old Brewery, 6 Blundell Street,
London N7 9BH, United Kingdom.
T (0)20 7700 6700 F (0)20 7700 8066
www.QuartoKnows.com

A catalogue record for this book is available from the British Library.

ISBN 978-0-7112-4429-0

Author: Simon Mugford
Series Editor: Joyce Bentley
Editor: Sasha Morton
Consultant: Helen Marron
Designer: Elaine Wilkinson

FSC MIX Paper from responsible sources FSC® C001701

Manufactured in Shenzhen, China PP062019

9 8 7 6 5 4 3 2 1

Photo Acknowledgments
Shutterstock: front cover, p6-7, 20 and 22 FamVeid; back cover and imprint page Samuel Borges Photography; title page, p18-19, 20 and 22 oliveromg; p3 and 8 vvita; p4-5 and 20 Alexander Raths; p5 and 20 Eric Gavaert; p9 Monkey Business Images; p10-11 and 22 Brocreative; p12 Evgeny Bakharev; p13 Jaromir Chalabala; p14-15 maxslu; p16-17 Anurak Pongpatimet; p17 Romrodphoto; p21Gelpi; p23t Sergiy Bykhunenko; p23b yvegeniy11

The sun is hot in summer.

The days are long and light.

We can play all day in summer.

The leaves go brown in autumn.

Animals need to look for food.

We can play in the autumn leaves.

Crunch!

Crunch!

The days are short and dark in winter.

We need hot drinks!

Snow in winter is the most fun of all.

18

Match it!

Follow the line from each picture
to read the word.

snow   rain   flowers   animals

Clap it!
Say the 'Match it!' words.
Clap the syllables.

Sound it!
Sound out each of these words.

| l o ng | l igh t | sh or t | f oo d |

Say it!
Read and say these words.

| to | all | are | we |

Describe it!

1 What is rain like?
What does rain feel like?
What sound does it make?

2 Describe what you can see in each of these pictures. How are they the same? How are they different?